Don't Forget the Courtesy Flush

I0484246

Don't Forget the Courtesy Flush

Dedicated to Vanessa.

I cannot thank you enough for the faith you show in me every day. You are my inspiration and my heart. You make me happy. You make me aspire to become a better man so that I can be worthy of your love.

Don't Forget the Courtesy Flush

Forward

In this book I am going to share with you some of the pitfalls I encountered by not having the right mindset.

From learned behaviors that do or do not contribute to a healthy outlook on work, business and life.

While you are enjoying the experiences that I am about to share, you may begin to see that there were times in your life that resulted in extraordinary growth, even though you may not have realized it at the time.

If even one sentence, paragraph or chapter resonates with you and causes you to make just a small shift toward a more powerful mindset then I will have accomplished my goal - *To help others avoid some of the challenges that I have had to overcome.*

Don't Forget the Courtesy Flush

People are always competing on social media it seems. Competing to get likes of their stuff and to get people to make friends with them. That is all fine and dandy but keep in mind that your true friends may be the ones who quietly sit and observe.

I consider myself fortunate to have grown up as an Army brat. The places I have been in my life are far beyond where most people will be able to travel in their lives.

But more important are the quality of friends that I have had the privilege to make. Friends that are like family. Some of them I have known for over 35 years and are really more like family. Without them I would not be where I am today.

Don't Forget the Courtesy Flush

You will soon see that many people have had a big impact on me. I would like to thank some of them now.

First and foremost thanks Mom and Dad. I do not know how you managed to keep your sanity or keep from just giving up on me. I love you more than life. Mom you taught me to look for the best in others and strive to be the best I can be. Dad, thanks for not killing me. I would have. I know I deserved it. Thanks for having patience and faith in me and becoming a great friend and role model. I can only hope that I can make you proud one day.

My sisters are next. Michelle, you set the bar high for me and I think that I have finally grown to deserve such a great role model. You kept the peace and were often a protector. Andrea, what can I say. We kid and joke but you always bring happy memories when I think of you. And you have also taught me some valuable lessons. Like stepping on a nail hurts. Thanks for that one. Also for discovering that Vick's VapoRub does NOT make a good shampoo but does keep your sinuses clear for a few weeks if you decide to use it that way.

Mark, you are my very best friend and will be for life. You are family. You are an inspiration and a hero to me and everyone who knows you. You and Cindy have instilled your courage and compassion in your children, a legacy that will continue for many generations.

Kay and Pam. You are like my sisters, I love you dearly. You have been my confidants on more than one occasion.

All of my old and dear friends that I have known since our time in

Don't Forget the Courtesy Flush

Germany, my thoughts often turn to you and my heart smiles.

There are so many more of you. Please know that though you may not be mentioned here you are no less important to me.

Thanks to Dave and Erin Sharpe, you enabled me to realize that my potential is far greater that I can know.

BJ Min, thanks for telling me to write this book.

To you who read this book, I hope that I can inspire you to believe in your abilities to succeed and inspire you to take the action that is required and to never, never, NEVER give up on your dreams.

Remember, If I can do this you can do anything you set your mind to.

Don't Forget the Courtesy Flush

Contents

Don't Forget the Courtesy Flush

Don't Forget the Courtesy Flush

Don't Forget the Courtesy Flush

Don't Forget the Courtesy Flush

The Earliest Memories are Lasting Ones

Don't you just love those videos. The ones where a soldier returning home surprises their loved one in school or at another event. We all do. They never fail to bring a tear of joy to my eyes.

We feel that way because we are empathetic beings. We love to be able to share the joy of other people. But there is another side to what those videos fail to convey.

Let me explain what I mean.

I have never shared this with anyone before so please bear with me.

I grew up in a military family

And I remember the last time my Dad got sent to war. I was 5 or 6 years old and he was being sent off to Viet-Nam for his 3rd tour. That is one of the earliest painful memories that I have.

I remember hugging him tightly and not letting go, saying that I did not want him to leave. As hard as that was for me I cannot even imagine how difficult it was for him. But he had signed up and was bound to fulfill his duties. I remember him telling me that he would be back soon and I was going to be the man around the house for a while. Trying to take my mind off the fact he was leaving and giving me a sense of pride with an important job to do by taking care of my mother and sisters in his absence.

We were fortunate

because my dad came back and had a great career in the Army.

Don't Forget the Courtesy Flush

While we have a great relationship now, it wasn't always that way. I think that I resented him for leaving me when I was such a young boy and carried that resentment into early adulthood. I resented it so much that I even grew to hate the color green.

Yes we love those homecoming videos, don't we?

But there is another untold side to those videos...

We never see the good bye videos

of a soldier trying to explain why he is going away to his young son or daughter.

We don't see the video of a soldier saying goodbye to his young, beloved wife. Assuring her that he will stay safe and return to her soon, all the while

knowing that he may never hold her again.

We don't want to hear or even admit or realize is that for some of them it will be the last time their families will see them as they are, physically or mentally. Or even worse, some are final goodbye's.

But even when a soldier does come back many may not be so fortunate. Especially today. With the military cutting back forces, soldiers are coming home having done their service and being 'let go'. Sent out into the world to recreate their lives.

I have a very high respect for those who have served our great country but I also believe that they should not have to struggle to make ends meet when they get out. I also know that there are countless spouses who want their soldiers to be safe and be able to stay at home.

Don't Forget the Courtesy Flush

I want to show them how they can do just that.

How they can create an online business that can allow them to out-process for good. They have done their service and now they have an option to build a business that will allow them to enjoy their families and freedoms that they fought so hard for.

Don't Forget the Courtesy Flush

All In - All Out

Have you been told to get all in?

It is kind of a catch phrase these days. But do you really know what it means?

Lots of people understand it and use it the wrong way and that can have disastrous results. The phrase comes from poker players meaning that they are putting all of their chips in on the bet.

When this is used in business many people use it as a pressure tactic for the purpose of making more money from prospective clients and associates who join them. When it is used in this way it is a recipe for failure. Sooner or later their methods will catch up to them and they themselves will be left without a dollar to their names.

The way that I believe it should be used and interpreted is a bit different. When

Don't Forget the Courtesy Flush

I ask someone if they are all in I will ask them several questions and then explain my question to them.

I believe that the context of the phrase "All In" should be used in regard to home business entrepreneurs, is not that they have bought every single product or service whether they could afford it or not. Rather it should be used to gauge a persons commitment of decision. Being all in should refer to a person being fully committed to their business.

Committed.

Committed to investing as much time as possible every day. This means that whether it is two hours or ten, a person needs to spend that time every day. They will spend that time on the activities and actions that are income producing activities. Not checking emails or Facebook or Youtube. Not texting with friends and family. It means treating their time as if they are getting paid by the hour in a job. This time will be spent marketing, recruiting and selling. That is about it. Writing an ad is not an income producing activity. Writing a blog post is not an IPA. Sending an email broadcast is not an IPA. Making a training or sales video is not an IPA. Marketing the videos and articles is an IPA. Syndication and publicizing are IPA's. Get the picture?

Committed to investing in their education about the business. They will set aside time to learning and taking the right actions every day in order to reach their goals. This is not to be included in the above time that is committed to business building. That time is for IPA's and training videos and audios are not income producing activities.

Committed to not quitting because of some lame excuse of not knowing how to do something or that they have not seen any results in the first day or week. If they want to just sit back and place one ad expecting that money will magically fall from the sky then they should not even get in at all. That is not how business works. It also does not work to just visualize making money, you need to take action.

Committed to personal growth. If they are not willing to grow personally as well, then their success will be hindered severely. Without personal growth it will be next to impossible to build and sustain a thriving business and team. Learning to respond to situations in order to learn and prosper from them instead of just knee jerk reactions guided by personal emotions and past experiences.

Committed to investing in as many products and services as possible as

Don't Forget the Courtesy Flush

soon as they can. When they do this they are increasing their potential earning power. By doing this you make it possible to market more and higher paying products. If they cannot do it right off the bat that is ok. Sometimes people really do not have the funds to invest. That being said they should commit to getting them as soon as possible. Think about it. How much faster can you make money by selling products that pay $350 than $18. At $18 you would need to make 20 times more sales than you would if you sold one $350 commission product. To be honest it is no more difficult to sell the higher priced product as it is to sell the lower priced one.

Committed to themselves. They can commit to you as much as you want them to and may never really mean anything to them. However, if you make them commit to themselves as well and do it in writing, you will have a much better chance of them following through with their promise. Remember, in most cases you will not have a personal connection with a new person joining your business. Both you and them have to work toward building rapport with one another. You as a leader who will guide them on a path and them to be accountable and responsible for taking the actions necessary to secure their own success. In turn they will need to become the leader and build rapport with their new team members.

Committed to their success. They must be committed to their success and obedient to a plan of action to get them there. Merely wanting to succeed does not allow the subconscious mind to work in your favor. Wanting is the same as trying. They are both failure oriented thoughts. If you try something you are saying to yourself that you do not believe that you will be able to succeed and your subconscious is already working on an excuse of why you failed. However a decision to succeed with no other possible outcome will set your subconscious in motion to bring resources and situations to you that will ensure that success. Your subconscious will also trigger the drive needed to recognize and act on decisions that need to be made.

So to me, being "All In" means that you are fully committed to your success emotionally and to the highest level financially possible. Being pressured to invest more money than you are able is not a good thing but you should invest at the highest level possible.

Now be prepared for the fact that those who are able to invest at a higher level will probably receive a higher level of training and when a team member who is able to invest to that higher level at a later date they will then get that same high level training. Groups and masterminds will also have minimum commitment levels in order to better serve those who have made higher levels of commitment. Leaders should attempt to create lower level groups in order to bring others up and along in their businesses.

If you are a leader you must remember that you were also at one time or another walking in the same shoes as those who are just getting started in their online business careers. Your compassion and encouragement can be the biggest help in a persons new business. showing that you believe they can be successful is invaluable.

I recall that over the years I never really had anyone who cheered me on. No one who wanted to see me succeed for a reason other than they would make money because of it. That is until I joined Empower Network. I have been encouraged by leaders who have no vested interest in my success other than bearing witness to the person I am becoming.

Don't Forget the Courtesy Flush

And of course the most important person to have in your corner, backing you up with true belief and love is your spouse or significant other.

Thank you Vanessa for believing in me.

That is what real leaders will do. That is what a real family does.

Don't Forget the Courtesy Flush

Don't Forget the Courtesy Flush

Who is making your decisions

While we were out riding and taking in the beautiful scenery last fall, I began to drift in my thoughts about how exactly I came to be at that particular spot at that particular time. I realized that there was a long list of events and decisions that I made in order to be where I was. Had I taken a different path years back or done something just a little different last week, chances are I would not have been on that horse.

A long time ago, I was reading an inspirational book, at this time I cannot even remember what the book was. In the book it went on to explain the decision making process of the average person and the ones who have an impact on this world and live life on their terms.

Don't Forget the Courtesy Flush

It went on to say that most people make decisions about non crucial issues based on information they gather from the opinions of their friends and peers. Think about that for a second. The last new restaurant you tried was probably because a friend raved about it.

But when it comes to crucial or "big" decisions that will actually make a difference in their lives is where the differences lie. The average person will rely on doing only minimal research and depend on the views and opinions of their peer group. They see a venture as a risk and do not trust their own decision making processes. They do this as a sort of safety mechanism. This way if something goes badly, they can dodge taking responsibility for the error but if all goes right they seldom give the credit to those who gave their opinions. If they decide against something then they can commiserate with their friends about wasn't it lucky for them they did not do it, or can blame someone else for their lot in life because they took so and so's advice and did not buy that Apple stock when it first came out.

Highly successful people are actually almost polar opposite. They readily take full responsibility for their actions and decisions from the get go. They rely only marginally on the opinions of others. They generally ask their peers about this or that but it is not really to find out their opinion about something but to gain insight about how it could most beneficial to them or their situation. Then they go about personally investigating and testing on a small scale. If their first test goes not so well they usually test again, making small adjustments and tweaks. Often times repeating this process many times before rejecting something, and sometimes a single test will merit going forward even though the test did not produce stellar results. It showed promise and they know that taking action will result in a big win or at the very least they will refine their process for the next time.

So, knowing that and where you are in your business, what decisions would you have made differently? Are you still relying on the opinions of others. If so take a good hard look at where those people are at. Are they leaders in the industry or your friends who are stuck in their jobs. Are you seeking the opinions of the winners or the losers?

Don't Forget the Courtesy Flush

Dig your own well

When I first started to market online I was always asking other people where they were getting their traffic and where they were posing their ads. I wanted to know the secret sources and methods they were using to succeed.

It is only natural to want to ask these questions of your sponsor or upline leaders. We all want to know the secret source of their success and by asking those questions we are demonstrating that we also want the success they are having.

That is what we all want.

When they don't give us the exact answer or we don't get the same results we want to blame them for our lack of results.

But here is the real answer.

Don't Forget the Courtesy Flush

You probably won't like it.

When I was on a training call a while back with a leader he eluded to this and he explained the reason why you will seldom get an exact answer. The first reason is because even if you do get their secret source of leads and traffic you will most likely NOT get the same kind of results they are getting. Then you will probably believe that they did not give you the true answer and will build a negative view of them when they have done nothing but try to help you.

The second answer follows the above reason. If they give you the answer you will lose out on learning how to cultivate your own resources. If you have to discover your own resources you will gain the experience and confidence you will need to become your own success story. When you have to do the leg work you make your own paths and contacts. You build your

Don't Forget the Courtesy Flush

own team of people who are loyal to you and who you can trust. You won't be concerned that your contacts or team gives preference to someone else above you.

That is digging your own well. You know the work it took to create it and the quality of water it delivers to you on a consistent basis.

So to get the most powerful results and exceed your biggest goals...

Dig your own well.

Don't Forget the Courtesy Flush

Don't Forget the Courtesy Flush

What fountain are you drinking from?

I just got a rather sad email in reply to a message sent from my autoresponder.

The email subject line was "Have you looked into Empower Network yet?"

The reply was this

I have and it is one the better companies around. It's just all those boats have sailed now and I can't see much of a future getting into this now. but yea empower are better than most. At least you have decent products.

regards
N#$%$ B@#$%#%

The reason why I found this to be so sad is because this man had apparently lost his dream and his hopes were dashed.

He agreed that the Company was solid and had a better track record than most companies and that the products were good.

He said that he had looked into joining previously.

Something had obviously stopped him.

But what I read was that something had made him stop believing in himself. With belief in his own abilities destroyed he lost his ability to see his dream.

He lost hope.

This makes me sad because it is something that we all have to battle from time to time. Something doesn't work out how we had hoped and we feel defeated. We begin to doubt if we

Don't Forget the Courtesy Flush

can really do this, do whatever it takes, to continue on. We open the door for that insidious demon of self doubt and if we are not vigilant it will continue to push and push until it has taken hold.

It will eat away at your confidence and self worth until you are empty of hope and your dream has faded from your heart and soul.

That is why when you are working in your business it is of utmost importance that you do not become attached to any specific outcome.

Treat it like a game.

Kinda like at the Casino. With one huge difference.

Instead of the odds being in favor of the house, they are in your favor.

You may lose one or two times but overall you will be the one winning.

Don't Forget the Courtesy Flush

And winning BIG!

All you need to do is continue to play.

That is what the Casino's do. They continue to deal the cards. They continue to play the games and though they may lose today over time their winnings are massive.
They are not attached to the outcome of a single game of Poker or a spin of the wheel. They have a' big picture' point of view and they know small losses lead to huge gains.

How long would they be in business if they lost a single game of black jack and just closed their doors?

But how long have they been in business?

To remain in business they have to be profitable, and they are among the most profitable businesses there are.

Don't Forget the Courtesy Flush

So just let go of the results from your single actions and view the results from a months, or 3 months worth of work. See your results no matter how small and take note of all improvements. They all add up to a picture of success.

You can focus on what did not happen OR you can focus on the improvements that were made. Either way your focus will become a self fulfilling prophecy for the results of your future.

So why not accentuate the positive!

Don't Forget the Courtesy Flush

Don't Forget the Courtesy Flush

Are you making excuses or money? You can't do both.

I recently had a conversation with a person who contacted me about their business.

After speaking with them for a minute I felt like something was a little bit off. It seemed like he was avoiding answering my questions.

They were not hard questions.
Actually they were pretty easy. You can get a list of the top questions to ask when recruiting here.

It seemed that all he wanted to do was complain and have a sounding board. He wanted someone to agree with his view of why he wasn't having any success in his business.

It was one after the next –

Don't Forget the Courtesy Flush

I can't get hold of my sponsor. No one will tell me the secret traffic source they are using. I don't have enough time to write a blog post every day. I can't figure out what to write about.

and on and on and on…

Every time I began to reply he would cut me off and throw out another objection as to why he was not making any money.

So I paused and let him rant for a while. After he blew off enough steam he paused a second and asked me "So what do you have to say about that?"

I remained silent for about 20 more seconds. Just as he began to speak again I interrupted him.

"Are you done?"

He began to speak again and again I interrupted him.

Don't Forget the Courtesy Flush

"Because if you are not I am going to hang up the phone because I am not going to waste my time listening to you go on and on complaining when you called me, wanting me to answer some questions. So I am going to ask you again and I just want a single word for an answer – Are you done? Yes or NO?"

He replied yes.

I then paused a few more seconds. Then I asked him a simple question.

What do you want from your business?

He was on track now and answered pretty quickly.

Our conversation went on and I was asking him questions so that I could find out what was causing his lack of success.

Then I asked him if he was on Facebook? He said yes. I got his page up and was surprised at what he had been doing.

I then asked him again how much time he was dedicating to his business. He said that he did a couple hours a day after he got home from work. I poked around on his page and noticed something that pretty much answered his questions.

While I was asking him the questions they were to figure out what was going on with his marketing. I asked where he had been doing his marketing and he told me that his favorite place was on Facebook.

When I asked him how often he placed an ad on Facebook he replied that he had put up about 4 in the past 2 months. Digging a bit more I found out that he had not really advertised but had boosted a few posts. I asked him how he was doing with candy crush. He gave me some level number that seemed high to me. Then I commented that he seemed to do pretty well with Trivia Crack. He proudly said that he was.

I then told him that I thought I had an answer to why he was not having the results he wanted. I told him that I would tell him only if he agreed to allow me to finish what I was going to say and not interrupt me.

He agreed.

Here is what I told him.

When I was asking you those questions after you agreed to work with me I was trying to find out where your marketing was going south. You answered that you only had a couple hours a night to work on your business and that you dedicated that time every night. You answered that your favorite advertising place was Facebook which is fine but the story that I saw when I looked on

Don't Forget the Courtesy Flush

your wall said something different and the answers you gave about the games you played confirmed what I saw on your wall.

What I noticed is that while you did dedicate those two hours every night they were not used in building your business.

He began to interrupt and I stopped him.

What I saw was that you posted your trivia game and candy crush many times and also commented on every ones funny little pictures and sayings. You wrote a rant here and there about football or basketball games or teams. You liked and shared loads o other peoples stuff but I did not see any marketing going on at all.

I asked if you were doing one on one marketing by starting up conversations with people. You said that you were not. I asked if you were using a blog to create content and promote your business – you said no.

So from what I have seen the reason why you are not getting the results that you want is that you are not doing anything to create ANY results. You are playing games and screwing around on Facebook but you are not doing anything to promote your business, but you have no problem blaming your lack of success on your sponsor being unavailable to you.

So if you had a person on your team that was not doing anything but wanted to take up your time and complain about not getting results would you make yourself available to them?

He started once again to offer up excuses and blame.

I stopped him – Yes or No!

Don't Forget the Courtesy Flush

He replied NO! and started again to justify his actions or inactions.

I stopped him again.

So you feel that you have the right to waste someone else time with complaining and BS but you would not put up with it yourself. Right?

He began to explain and justify again and I stopped him one final time.

Well I won't accept it either and hung up.

In the past I might have let someone waste my time with stuff like that and been afraid to tell them what I saw for fear of hurting their feelings and losing a possible sign up. But I have since learned that in order for others to respect me and my time I had to respect my time and myself first by not giving or taking BS excuses from myself or anyone else.

Don't Forget the Courtesy Flush

I know that I didn't give you a blow by blow version but just a short and sweet version.

But I have a question for you. Do you think I handled that right? Would you let someone waste your time like that? What would you have done differently?

Don't Forget the Courtesy Flush

Don't Forget the Courtesy Flush

Smashing the barriers

Are you ready for your breakthrough?

Are you ready to get past what has you stuck?

The best way I have found to do that, is to break down the barriers that are keeping you from your success. Would you agree with that? I know that sounds like a stupid question but just go with me on this for a sec.

When you want to get past whatever it is that is blocking your success then you have to do one of 4 things.

1. go around it

2. go over it

3. go under it

4. GO THROUGH IT!

Don't Forget the Courtesy Flush

We all know that right?

But did you know that you already know what you need to do?

You already have the knowledge to smash any roadblock in your way.

You may need some more tools but you have the knowledge.

You just need to ask yourself a different set of questions. A mentor of mine, Ray Higdon wrote an article that may also help you. Not only ask different questions but your answers need to be different as well.

What do I mean by that?

I mean that instead of blaming a failed campaign on something or someone, how about you look at it just a little different. Not as a failure but as a stepping stone, an example of something to avoid in the future.

Don't Forget the Courtesy Flush

When I was 16, I was a Black Belt in Tae Kwon-do. I was an assistant instructor for our school. I was also on a German fighting team and had a Brown Belt in Shotokan Karate.

I was practicing 5 nights a week, at least 3 hours a night. Two nights were at our school and the other three were for the fighting team.

Weighing in at about 130 lbs and 6'1" I was very fast and because I was 16, fearless.

One evening I woke up on the floor *looking up at my instructor. He was about 6'3", 250 lbs.*

We would generally get a early start on our classes and put in an hour of stretching and sparring because we didn't have much time to do so when we were teaching. This day we were sparring and he knocked me out cold.

Don't Forget the Courtesy Flush

As I came to, I was wondering what happened. What did I miss?

He showed me exactly what he did and explained what happened. I nodded and told him he better watch out next time.

He watched for the next 7 times we sparred together.

I kept missing the show.

Then one day everything changed.

I hadn't planned anything in particular but was really in the zone. When he made his famous "Knock Dave Out" move I just reacted automatically. I spun around and without even realizing it I had eluded his strike and moved in with a counter strike.

CRACK!

Then I stopped in mid attack.

Don't Forget the Courtesy Flush

He had fallen to one knee and was holding his nose. He looked up at me with a smile on his face and said "help me get to the locker room".

With blood flowing from his nose and not being able to see I guided him to the sink where he looked in the mirror and with his nose between both hands he pressed.

Crunch! He straightened it out and said "Now I want to show you what you did, because I know you don't realize how you did this"

He was right. He told me that I had spun out and around his attack and was going to strike him with a spinning back-fist to his head. He said that it was so quick that he did not have time to react except to turn his head a bit and my elbow just caught his nose with a glancing blow.

Don't Forget the Courtesy Flush

I had learned what my problem was,

but as hard as I tried, I couldn't fix it.

I kept doing this or that. I even knew what was coming I just didn't know when.

By focusing on the problem I was unable to recognize the events that were leading up to it and therefore kept getting the exact same result. My instructor had noticed a pattern or ' tell' in my style that allowed him to take advantage of an opening.

He even told me exactly what it was and how he was doing what he was doing.

I could have just blamed him for "playing too hard" or taking advantage of a situation but that would have kept me from growing through the problem.

Don't Forget the Courtesy Flush

He was not meaning to knock me out all the time but I kept **walking in to his attack**

- with my face –

- resulting in the lights going out.

The night that I avoided his attack for the first time and broke his nose was not because I had learned some cool new technique or method. It was actually just by doing what was a very basic move taught to beginning students, and practiced many, many times. When I got past trying to stop his attack and focused on fighting I was able to see it coming as if in slow motion and my reaction was so simple. By making a half step to the side and a half turn I changed the outcome completely.

By focusing on the larger picture you will be able to recognize what may need to be adjusted to change your outcome. Just like I did when I was 16.

Sometimes we need to step back and see the bigger picture and the solution will present itself. It can be hard to do when you are stuck in a cycle of bad results. It can be so easy to blame it on this or that and just chalk it up as another failure.

But if you just change your mindset and focus, the solution may just be even easier than you think. It could be something as simple as going through a training for the fourth time or even reading a book. You can also invest in yourself by getting coaching and mentoring by a person you trust and admire. I have been able to do this with a mentor of mine, Dave Sharpe. I am not sure when he will do it again but feel free to contact me if you are interested in learning more.

Don't Forget the Courtesy Flush

It could be something as simple what is being said and how is it being said? Do you see something that you could model here? Is there something that may just be the key to what you need to unlock?

Maybe…

Don't Forget the Courtesy Flush

Don't Forget the Courtesy Flush

IT's just a small shift away...

What is IT?

Do you really want to know?

IT is your success, and your success starts with a small shift in the language you use with yourself and everyone else you come in contact with.

When I heard Ray Higdon say that I scoffed – silently of course – and sat there with my arms crossed. I was thinking to myself Ray, who the hell do you think you are! You have no idea what kind of language I use. I am quite articulate.

Ray kept talking,

"You know something, there is no coincidence that you are here today listening to me. You are here for a reason and that is to learn something.

Don't Forget the Courtesy Flush

And once you learn this you are responsible. You cannot unlearn this. You cannot unhear this! You are responsible for taking action. Because you will know what to do. You will then be responsible for applying it or owning it to yourself and the world that in reality you are happy in your failures and mediocrity and do not want to become successful after all."

When Ray said this it really hit home and I began to listen "When you justify where you are, you stay where you are. And when you justify where you are you will win the booby prize – smallness!"

Well since that day I have decided to move forward with the knowledge he gave me because I know that only I am responsible for ME!(he was right) I did not want to build a mountain of smallness I want Greatness! I do not want you to play small either. When you play small you are settling. You are accepting that you do not deserve to have anything better than where you are at.

Are you ready to learn what is holding you back?

It is you.

Not your family, *not* your spouse, *not* your neighbors, *not* your past **or** ***anything else that does not use your brain to think.***

And that is the first step. Use your brain to think for yourself and take charge.

Remember, once you hear the truth you cannot unhear or unlearn it. You are stuck with it. You then have to face the real you.

Don't Forget the Courtesy Flush

The turning point

After 17 years

away from Tae Kwon-Do I decided to get back into it. I knew that returning as a second dan blackbelt was not going to happen, the instructor said that I could come back in as a Blue belt and at the next test he would decide what level I would continue at. After about a month in the class I was going for a belt test that I thought was a red belt.

I was set up to spar with a guy I had never met and with all the gear on I couldn't get a good read on him. This was the beginning of the testing day and sparring is one of my favorite activities.

The set up was a little strange to me because there were about 10 matches going on all at once. The Dojo was not very large so space was at a premium. I squared off with my opponent and on a

Don't Forget the Courtesy Flush

clap of hands from our instructor we began.

From past experiences

of fighting in Germany at tournaments I knew that making an aggressive and fast first move was key to winning the mind game of a match. I kicked fast and pulled the kick as soon as I made contact with the chest guard, making a very loud pop sound but not hitting hard.

When my opponent cowered

and began to cry is when I noticed that he was mentally challenged. I stopped immediately and went to him to calm him. I comforted him and asked him if he was hurt. He responded that he was not hurt but was scared by the loud sound of the kick striking his chest protector.

Don't Forget the Courtesy Flush

I talked with him for a minute in a 2 man huddle in the midst of all the chaos. I got him to smile and giggle a bit and then asked if he wanted to learn how to make that loud pop when he kicked or punched. He smiled very big and looked into my eyes saying that he would. We proceeded to spar and I was being his live punching bag.. Giving him pointers of how to see his openings and how to strike fast and make the loud sound when he contacted his opponent.

By the time the session was over he was identifying the openings I was leaving and was striking fast and making that loud sound that had scared him so much. We bowed to each other and then he hugged me and went to sit back on the sidelines smiling from ear to ear. I, on the other hand was stunned and was left standing dumbfounded in the middle of the mat with a tear welling up in my eye.

Don't Forget the Courtesy Flush

Because I was focusing on me

when we started I did not recognize what my opponent needed. I was in fight mode like it was a tournament. I did not realize that my instructor had seen that I had the skills needed to perform all of the moves and forms.

I was being tested on my abilities to lead and teach. When I stopped and comforted my sparring partner in the middle of the test, ignoring my own performance that I thought I was testing for was when I passed my test. The rest of the day I spent sitting and watching all the other students perform their forms and moves and breaking their boards. I was not called to do anything else.

At the end of the test

everyone else had gone up and received their new belts I thought that I had failed miserably. I thought that because

Don't Forget the Courtesy Flush

I had ignored the testing procedure and stopped fighting and went into teaching mode that I had embarrassed the instructor and that I would be put back down to white belt to start all over again.

But then when I thought that the ceremony was over our instructor stood in front of the class and audience. Silent for a moment, looking over the students proudly wearing their new belts. He then turned to the audience and looked at them. Looking at them all from one side to the other, silently.

He began to speak.

He explained that there was a very special test going on that day that he had not told anyone about. He said that in the very beginning he had a serious concern whether he had done the right thing. Then what he had hoped for happened.

Don't Forget the Courtesy Flush

He said that he saw complete disregard

of his outlined and acceptable testing format, and saw compassion. He explained that one person was not being tested as they thought they were. He said that one person was not being tested on skill or form. That person was being tested on his ability to disregard his own needs and focus on the needs of another. That person was being tested on his ability to lead.

When he called me up I was floored and even more surprised when he bowed deeply to me and tied a Black Belt around my waist

I did not ever realize the power

of it until the other day. I was on a webinar training with Chris. For years I had been comfortable being the guy with potential. I had shifted my focus to myself. I had developed a " look at me

Don't Forget the Courtesy Flush

" attitude and my results sowed it. I had to focus on the other person, to their needs before I could grow any more.

When I looked back I realized that every time I put my mind to something I just did whatever it took. I removed me from the equation and focused on the result. The result of what I really desired rather than what I wanted monetarily, is when I have had the best outcome. Just like I had when I went into automatic teaching mode, wanting that young man to succeed and step into a bravery that he had never known and unconsciously disregarding the acceptable procedures and how I would do on the test. That is it. Focus on providing what your customer needs and what you want will be presented to you.

Don't Forget the Courtesy Flush

Faith and Answers From God

Perhaps you have been saying to yourself that you need to hear from a higher power before you start down a business path or that you need to pray on it. I think that it is great that people have faith in a higher power. It does not matter if you refer to it as Jesus, God, Allah, Buddah or any other name you may wish to use. But have you ever considered that the answer to what you are seeking is being delivered through the person you are saying these things to.

If you have been asking for guidance about how to create a better life for you and your family, perhaps the invitation to a business presentation is the sign you are praying for. I was raised catholic so forgive the following phrase and use it in a context that works for you – The Lord Works in Mysterious Ways!

The way I see it is that He answers our prayers and requests and it is up to us to recognize the messages He is sending. It reminds me of a joke that has an eye opening punch line that I feel could be helpful.

A religious man is on top of a roof during a great flood. A man comes by in a boat and says "get in, get in!" The religous man replies, " no I have faith in God, he will grant me a miracle."

Later the water is up to his waist and another boat comes by and the guy tells him to get in again. He responds that he has faith in god and god will give him a miracle. With the water at about chest high, another boat comes to rescue him, but he turns down the offer again cause "God will grant him a miracle."

With the water at chin high, a helicopter throws down a ladder and they tell him to get in, mumbling with the water in his mouth, he again turns down the request for help for the faith of God. He arrives at the gates of heaven with broken faith and says to Peter, I thought God would grand me a miracle and I have been let down." St. Peter chuckles and responds,

Don't Forget the Courtesy Flush

"I don't know what you're complaining about, we sent you three boats and a helicopter."

So in your faith

that your higher power or God will give you answers, keep in mind that the answers are being given to you all the time. However they are seldom what we envision. There will probably NOT be a choir of angels on high sounding trumpets in the golden rays of the heavens. You probably will NOT hear a powerful echoing voice from the heavens telling you answers to what you are asking about. You probably will NOT see a vision of him or her floating above the ground in a mystical halo of light.

Don't Forget the Courtesy Flush

Rather than being a burning bush or a booming voice from the heavens, it will more likely be just an average person inviting you to try something new, sharing what has worked for them. Or if you still insist on waiting at least you will have your something or someone to blame your lack of success on. – Just don't be surprised when St. Peter laughs at you.

Mastering Your Mindset

Have you ever felt like you are the only person online who isn't making money. If you are normal you have probably felt that way before or are feeling that way now. I know that I did for a long time. I was in online businesses for about 6 years without ever even making a cent.

It was lonely and discouraging

figuring out all the things I needed to know. I had to learn how to put a blog up and install the plugins and get them all working together. I had to learn that I needed an autoresponder and my own capture pages. Of course I didn't find all this out at one time. It was over the years. One piece at a time.

The one thing that I never needed to learn was feeling that I could make it in the online. I say feeling because I still had a big hurdle to get over. From the years of not achieving the results I wanted and being surrounded by people with negative attitudes and mentalities, I had lost *belief* that it was going to work for me. Fortunately I am a pretty stubborn guy. So I kept plugging away. I was just missing something and I knew that I would find it sooner or later.

In 2012 I Found what I needed. I also lost things. The losses of divorce, losing contact with friends, my home and way of life were gone. The things that remained and those that I found

Don't Forget the Courtesy Flush

have allowed me to become a better person. I found Vanessa who has been a huge part of my live and my biggest cheerleader, a source of inspiration and encouragement. I reinvented ME.

I still have hard days when I feel like nothing goes right. I guess everyone does. But I also have a lot of really great days. Those great days are the result of who and what has come into my life in the last two years. It seems that more and more often things just happen or show up that bring more and more success to me.

A lot of it I can attribute to my cheerleader, Vanessa.

There is not a day that goes by when she does not lift my spirits, make me laugh and give her support and encouragement. Through this coldest part of the year she forges on tackling a huge job of caring for her animals and maintaining her small farm. She is also only a couple of classes away from completing her degree. Knowing she is doing all that makes me realize that having a passion that drives you makes anything possible.

What is your passion?

What is it that gets you up in the morning and going to a job that you hate? What makes you endure hours of traffic? What makes you dream?

If you don't know then what are you doing?

Find your passion. If you don't know how, then I may have a way that will work for you. It takes a little time and a lot of thought, but it will be the best thing you can do for your future. Once you have found your passion you will be amazed at how things begin to fall into place that will work to get you closer to your goals.

Don't Forget the Courtesy Flush

What is the best language to speak

Are you bi-lingual? If you are that is great. But do you really know the question I just asked you?

Let me ask another way. What is the language you use when conducting your business?

Did you figure it out yet?

When you start a business do you plan to fail? I bet you don't.

Do you sometimes think that things are difficult or that you just don't know how or what to do. Don't get discouraged, it happens to all of us.

A while back I decided that I needed to learn another language in order to become successful. It was challenging but learning to speak this new language made it easier every day.

Confused yet.

OK, let me explain what I am really talking about.

The language that I am talking about is the self talk that we all have. I never realized how the language that I was using was actually perpetuating the difficulties that I was having. Then one day I was listening to an audio and I had a light bulb moment. I had been saying to myself that it was hard to figure out what to write about or I am just not good at doing videos or I get so confused or any other of the many things that we tend to say when we are having troubles with something.

In the audio it said that when we say something is difficult then our subconsious will work to make us right.

Don't Forget the Courtesy Flush

Rather than searching for ways to make things easier it is finding and inventing ways to keep the task difficult. It becomes a self-fulfilling prophecy.

Whether you think you can or you think you can't, you are absolutely right.

— Henry Ford

You see, our subconscious minds always work to make sure we are congruent with what we say, think and feel. So if we think that it is always hard to pick a subject to write about then it will be. But if we learn to speak a little differently it will soon begin to turn things around for us.

Take this for a test drive

Instead of – its always hard to think about what to blog about

Don't Forget the Courtesy Flush

change it to – The new Kalatu blog 21 day challenge plugin makes it easier and easier to find valuable things to write about.

Instead of – It's too scary to do a video.

change it to – Every tine I do a video it gets easier and easier to do and I get more comfortable every time.

Instead of – I can't write a good email to my list

change it to – Wow, The emails that I write are really getting better every day.

Instead of – I can't figure out how to …

change it to – New challenges are exciting and I learn how to do things quickly because I am such a smart person.

Don't Forget the Courtesy Flush

Instead of – I just don't have the time to do ...

Change it to – Because I am so good at managing my time I always have time to do the things that are necessary to ...

Get the hint?

One of the most important things that you need to master is your language, and your self talk needs to be first on the list.

If I had not been listening to the Inner Circle audios I fear that I would still be making those same self sabotaging statements that I had been using when i felt something was difficult. That is one of the many reasons that I made a commitment to myself to listen to personal development audios for at least an hour every day. The best thing that I have learned is that it can actually be a passive kind of thing. I can do it while I am driving, cutting the grass,

Don't Forget the Courtesy Flush

taking a shower, exercising or any other activity that you want.

Don't Forget the Courtesy Flush

What Would Happen if You Just Ask

Student asks if he could accompany Billy Joel. You can see the video at the link below.

https://www.youtube.com/watch?feature=player_embedded&v=Bceuh8c-4kg

The results were amazing.

Even Billy Joel was surprised. Just think of what we all would have missed if the student didn't work up the courage to ask.

When we are starting out in our online marketing careers, we try to do so many things and often feel like we are just never quite getting it right. So often in the beginning that is the case but we learn the tricks of the trade and start seeing little successes.

Don't Forget the Courtesy Flush

While it is all a part of the learning experience and "paying your dues" so to speak there is one HUGE thing that most marketers that are not having much success fail to do.

Just as shown in the video there are only two outcomes that can occur if you ask for the sale. They either buy or they do not. One thing is for sure...

If you do not ask, they will not buy from you and will end up buying from someone else who shows the confidence in their business and more importantly, themselves!

What are your thoughts about this? Do you find it difficult to ask for the sale? Are you going to keep struggling

OR

Are you going to take charge and finally do what it takes to succeed?

Don't Forget the Courtesy Flush

Get Out Of Your Own Way

The thing that is stopping "YOU" from succeeding is "YOU".

You are the reason why "YOU" are where "YOU" are and if you don't get up and do something, "YOU" will stay in the same unsatisfying spot you are in today!

Period!

It's your hurts, habits and hang-ups that are killing your success. That may not be what you want to hear but I am not here to tell you what you want to hear. You are reading this to find out how to become a successful online entrepreneur. That is the information I give to you with every paragraph and chapter that I write.

No BS.

No Fluff.

Don't Forget the Courtesy Flush

It is not easy to hear that but almost everyone that is successful has been there. I hope that you are willing to put away your ego for just a bit and hear me out.

We try to learn everything about a product or service and then we get uneasy about telling others about what we have to offer them. We are afraid of what they may say to us or about us behind our backs. You will not be able to please everyone and there will always be haters out there.

Maybe it's your best friend or a family member. That stings even more. I know I have been told on many occasions that I should just settle in and work for retirement. But then I see what is going on in the world and realize that I have to do something else because I will not be able to survive on what I will be able to build. Even if I could, how can I be sure that I won't get downsized or a pension/retirement fund won't be taken away by either the government or an employer?

Get up and DO something!

Live your dreams and fulfill your purpose!

Thomas Jefferson said:
"It is not the critic who counts; not the man who points out how
the strong man stumbles, or where the doer of deeds could have done them better.
The credit belongs to the man who is actually in the arena, whose face is marred by dust and sweat and blood; who strives valiantly; who errs, who comes short again and again, because there is no effort without error and shortcoming; but who does actually strive to do the deeds; who knows great enthusiasms, the great devotions; who spends himself in a worthy cause; who at the best knows in the end the triumph of high achievement, and who at the worst, if he fails, at least fails while daring greatly, so that his place shall never be with

Don't Forget the Courtesy Flush

those cold and timid souls who neither know victory nor defeat. "

Whoever it is that you are letting control your desires and decisions please know that the only power that they really have is what you give to them. They may honestly think that they are giving you good advice and they may mean well but the fact is your fear is allowing them to steal your dreams. Until you are ready to take back control and take action to build your dreams they will continue to control your life.

They only have the power that you give to them.

Are you ready to live life on your terms?

Are you prepared to take full

responsibility for your life? win or lose?

Well I guess I should let you in on a little secret.

If you choose to take full responsibility and commit to your dreams and vision and never give up then…

YOU CANNOT LOSE!

Don't Forget the Courtesy Flush

Don't Forget the Courtesy Flush

Get Free Rent ...

A recent post that I made on my blog had a few comments. I generally do not care what people say as long as they keep it clean. Unfortunately one fellow missed that mark a bit.

I had written about how on my journey through internet marketing I had been taken in by a few things and that sometimes there were people who were promoting a new launch every other day and that it seemed like there was a big ring of gurus that would do just that.

Any way this one guy I had apparently offended quite a bit. I was not selling anything just broadcasting a post. Well this guy just went off the deep end with a rant of how I should keep my thoughts to myself and those who cared and then he made it abundantly clear that he did not care! (that is the clean and short version.)

Don't Forget the Courtesy Flush

I guess he was one of those guys who did just that(the guru launch ring thing). I kind of think its funny that he took so much time and effort to craft such an abrasive and profane reply about something that he did not care about at all.

HAHAHAHA!

So just don't let the dimwits get you down.

If they truly did not care they would just ignore the post and move on.

When they do comment like this guy did, they are mad because you have shone a light upon a part of their own selves that they are trying to hide from others.

The best part is. You can just delete their reply and they will rant and rave to all their friends about your article, some of whom will read it and some

Don't Forget the Courtesy Flush

will even like it. Their friends know they are blowhards, and you get to live, RENT FREE in the empty space between their ears.

NEVER let someone else kill your vision. You are better than that.

Don't Forget the Courtesy Flush

Don't Forget the Courtesy Flush

A Lesson I Learned From Napoleon Hill

In his book "Think and Grow Rich", Napoleon Hill explained the difference between features and benefits as they relate to marketing. Of course I already knew the difference but what I missed was the reason why he was explaining it.

As a marketer I always wanted to just regurgitate facts – features – about how my vitamins were better or that the juice was more purple. Later I figured out what Hill was saying.

You see when you just overload people with facts and figures you are well on your way to losing a possibly otherwise loyal lifetime customer. Your customer does not really care about those things. What they really care about is what your product or service will do for them. How will it make their situation better. How it will ease their pain. These are the benefits that we need to show our customers.

There is a saying that goes "They do not care how much you know until they know how much you care". So if we just show our customers how much better their lives will be by using your products they will pay any price to have it.

Build trust and show that their needs and interests are what is important and they will buy from you even if someone else has the same product for cheaper. They will trust you and when they trust you they trust your judgment and recommendations to help them through their troubles.

One of the best ways to build trust

and show that you are not just after your customers money is to provide them with meaningful and helpful articles, videos, guides and other content.

I have had many people ask what was the best way to do that and my reply is a blog. With a blog you can provide all of these kinds of helpful content and bring it to them in their favorite social media platforms like Google Plus, FaceBook or twitter.

When people ask me where the best kind of blog is I will tell them what I am about to tell you.

Its right here. Just enter the link below and you will have the opportunity to have one of the most powerful blogging platforms available.

http://iwantto.getakalatu.website/

When you get there, fill out the form and get started now. I will even remove any risk for you by giving you a 14 day 100% money back guarantee.

Don't Forget the Courtesy Flush

You have nothing to lose and loads of loyal customers to gain so get started now.

After you get started shoot me an email and I will send you a link for your FREE copy of Napoleon Hills "Think and Grow Rich". I am sure that you will find loads of valuable ideas to share with your customers.

Overcoming Challenges and Roadblocks

I was recently involved in a challenge. It was a 21 day video challenge. On about day 4 or so I was also presented with another challenge that I felt was a bit more important and wanted to participate in. I didn't realize it then but the resolve that I had when I began the Video Challenge was something quite powerful.

When I began the second challenge, I said to myself that because I felt it was so much more important I would place my main focus on it and the video challenge would be secondary. With that in mind I immediately lost about 3 days in the video challenge.

I was feeling kind of guilty for losing ground but figured oh well there will be another one. About a day later I found that I had made a video that I had forgotten about and decided to edit and publish it because I figured it may get me back on track. When I published it and went to document my progress in the challenge group something clicked. It was that a lot of other people had also fallen behind but there were a few that had kept up. I knew that we could use makeup days in the challenge and decided that I would catch up an finish.

When I made that decision

I did not think that I would complete the *challenge* on time and wondered how I would do it and if the second project I was working on would suffer. In the past I would have felt overwhelmed at this point and would have begun to flounder.

Having my attention divided between two tasks that were important to me was the key to a lot of things I had never before realized.

Don't Forget the Courtesy Flush

After just 2 weeks of not only having completed both challenges, but completing them both ON TIME, I saw that my determination had paid off.

If you had read any of my articles about the first few months I had in this business, you know that I saw this as an opportunity to reinvent myself.

With fits and starts,

failures and successes, losses and wins, I had literally crushed many of the barriers that in the past would have resulted in just giving up and looking for something new.

I guess my determination showed through because looking back over the past year or so I can now see many things that are truly amazing. Although I was determined all along, I resisted a lot of things along the way that I now see. I will list a few of them below.

Don't Forget the Courtesy Flush

Some of my pitfalls...

- ***I had a "I already know that mentality"***
This kept me from growing personally and in my business. By learning a bit of humility and letting go of ego I have been able to just take the advice of people who were freely giving it and apply it in my business. When I decided to just listen to what they were saying, drop my preconceived beliefs and follow their instructions and guidance, I learned that they were actually telling me the truth. I learned that I alone was the one who could change my results. I just wish it hadn't taken me so long to realize it.

- ***Defining my vision.***
When I finally gave in, sat down and put some serious thought and effort into defining my vision and

goals things began to get a lot easier. When you have a clear and definite purpose tasks seem to fall into place without even thinking about them twice. Because I now know what I want, it is pretty easy to stay focused on individual tasks without getting distracted. When there are times when I need to interrupt what I am doing it is quite simple to pick right back up where I had left off and never miss a beat.

- ***Having a never quit mentality***
  Over the past year and a half there were times that I felt like I was never going to be able to put the pieces together and make an online business work. There were times when I doubted my ability to make it happen. But through it all I had people backing me up and cheering me on. Reminding me of what I had promised to myself. My Vision was

my driving force.

- ***It's ok to keep on going if you miss a target date or goal.***
  I used to feel like if I missed a goal or target date that I had failed. I now feel differently about those minor setbacks. Now I view them as stepping stones on my path to success. I no longer fear making a mistake or not reaching a goal on time. I just readjust my plan and carry on. I know that without action there will be no chance to succeed and fearing these little roadblocks will prevent me from taking any action and that is worse than a little misstep, that is resigning without ever having tried. Michael Jordan is one of the greatest athletes in history as far as I am concerned but he is far more than that. He is an inspirational role model. Did you know that he did not even make his

high school basketball team. What if he had let that kill his dream.

Here are a few of Michael Jordan's own words

that I think are important enough to share with you here.

Some people want it to happen, some wish it would happen, and others make it happen.

I've missed more than 9000 shots in my career. I've lost almost 300 games. 26 times, I've been trusted to take the game winning shot and missed. I've failed over and over and over again in my life. And that is why I succeed.

Don't Forget the Courtesy Flush

Obstacles don't have to stop you. If you run into a wall, don't turn around and give up. Figure out how to climb it, go through it, or work around it.

If you quit ONCE it becomes a habit. Never quit!!!

- Michael Jordan

What I have realized is that the commitment I made to myself is what has led to the success I have in my business today. By making that single commitment to follow the core commitments that have been laid out I have grown and taken a whole new attitude.

The things that have made the biggest change

Don't Forget the Courtesy Flush

for me were the commitments of listening to positive thinking and mindset training for at least 30 minutes daily, reading for an hour every day and going through some kind of training for building my business every day.

If you feel like you are floundering in business and the setbacks are making you doubt yourself, remember that you will likely have more failures along the way but every one brings you one step closer to success. Finding a proven system that guides you through to your level of desired success is the best and quickest way to get there.

Don't Forget the Courtesy Flush

Don't Forget the Courtesy Flush

Comments

Love this! You made me remember the times I was focused on other people and helping them succeed...is when I was the most successful myself. I've had "me" in the equation for quite a while recently and your message has been received. Thank you!

Charlene

Awesome Dave! I admire you for stepping back in to Taekwondo. It has been about 16 years since I was actively a Black Belt Instructor in Taekwondo. I loved it! Your automatic teaching mode prevailed....leadership skills revealed! Keep up the great work! Thanks for sharing your inspiration.

Sherry S

Don't Forget the Courtesy Flush

Great work Dave. Just goes to show once the decision was made to start the challenge no matter what obstacles(the weekend) were presented you found a way. A lesson more marketers need to learn Thanks for sharing Cheers!

Dale G

Wonderful writing, yes I agree, focus on the positive!

Annalise

Like you, I've been blogging for a long time and after hearing Neal speak I realized I was doing it all wrong! I've started implementing his strategies immediately. One thing I'm excited about is not having to spend a lot of time on SEO or keyword research. Yah!

Evan